LEGO® STAR WARS™

ROGUES AND VILLAINS

WRITTEN BY HANNAH DOLAN, ELIZABETH DOWSETT,
CLARE HIBBERT, SHARI LAST, AND VICTORIA TAYLOR

INTRODUCTION

Bounty hunters and villains cause trouble accross the LEGO® *Star Wars* galaxy. Find out about this dangerous group—from the deadly Darth Maul to the greedy Hondo Ohnaka.

Introduction
MEET THE MINIFIGURES

HOW TO USE THIS BOOK

These amazing minifigures are ordered according to the *Star Wars*™ property in which they first appeared or mostly featured. Tabs at the top of each page indicate which properties this minifgure appears in. As most *Star Wars* characters appear in the wider universe of Legends, that tab is highlighted only if a minifigure appears in an Legends set. The Clone Wars tab has not been highlighted if the character has a separate Clone Wars minifigure.

This book also includes variants of featured minifigures, which are the same character, but have some modifications that make them different in some way.

Contents

Darth Maul is the terrifying Sith apprentice of Darth Sidious. He lurks in the shadows, waiting for his chance to attack the Jedi! Maul's minifigure appears in nine LEGO *Star Wars* sets. His horned Zabrak head-mold was created in 2011, and in his 2012 variant he is without his usual robes—so you can see the Nightbrother tattoos on his arms.

Merry Sithmas
The 2012 LEGO *Star Wars* Advent Calendar came with a Santa Maul. He wears a red cape with a fur-lined hood, and has a festive candy cane printed on the back of his torso.

STAR VARIANTS

The eyes have it
Early Maul minifigures have regular LEGO® heads printed with Nightbrother tattoos and yellow eyes. This 1999 variant from Sith Infiltrator (set 7663) has black pupils in the eyes and different face patterns.

All in black
This 2011 minifigure appears in Darth Maul's Sith Infiltrator (set 7961). At the time, only two minifigures had double-bladed lightsabers: Maul and Savage Opress.

Darth Maul is a Nightbrother from Dathomir. His eyes have turned yellow from studying the dark side

In the first set to include Darth Maul—Lightsaber Duel (set 7101)—Maul's lightsaber hilt came with only one blade

This minifigure was used for promotional giveaways, including at the 2012 New York Toy Fair and LEGOLAND® Windsor in April 2012

New torso piece unique to this minifigure

Darth Maul
SITH APPRENTICE

DATA FILE
YEAR: 2012
FIRST SET: 5000062 Darth Maul
NO. OF SETS: 1
PIECES: 4
ACCESSORIES: Double-bladed lightsaber

Bounty Hunter Pursuit (set 7133)
Zam flies her nimble airspeeder in just this one 2002 set. The speeder's cockpit has a small control panel for Zam's navigation.

Dark gray LEGO flying goggles also appear on Podracers, Naboo Fighter Pilots, Gasgano and a variant of Anakin.

This shady character has proven elusive in LEGO *Star Wars* and her minifigure is exclusive to one 2002 set. Zam Wesell is a bounty hunter with a special edge: she is a Clawdite shapeshifter who can alter her physical appearance as she chooses. Her minifigure head can change between her pretty human disguise and her natural Clawdite face!

Heavy helmet
Zam's crash helmet is seen only on her minifigure in LEGO *Star Wars*. However, it is also used as a heavy-duty helmet by miners in the LEGO themes Power Miners and Rock Raiders, and by a driver in the World Racers theme. Only Zam wears it in light gray.

Face veil disguises Zam's human identity

Internal comlink for communicating with associates, including Jango Fett

Zam's torso, hips, and legs, printed with her specialized armor and equipment, are unique to her minifigure

Zam is the only minifigure that has ever been made in sand-purple

Grappling hook for scaling buildings

Zam Wesell
BOUNTY HUNTER

Changeling
Swiveling Zam's head around exposes her true Clawdite form. Zam was one of the first double-faced minifigures.

DATA FILE

YEAR: 2002
FIRST SET: 7133 Bounty Hunter Pursuit
NO. OF SETS: 1
PIECES: 5
ACCESSORIES: Rifle

Bounty hunter Jango Fett keeps a low profile in the LEGO *Star Wars* galaxy. He stars in just three sets, undergoing a redesign in 2013 for his appearance in Corporate Alliance Tank Droid (set 75015). Jango is made up of many unique LEGO pieces that might make his minifigure as legendary as the man himself.

Silver helmet with antenna has a printed black T-visor (the 2002 variant's has an opening)

STAR VARIANTS

Original Jango
The 2002 Jango defends *Slave I* (set 7153) with a pair of WESTAR-34 blaster pistols. His J-12 jetpack and helmet are one piece.

Santa's bounty
Jango wears red for his Santa variant in the 2013 LEGO *Star Wars* Advent Calendar (set 75023). He has presents tucked into his belt and holly on his chest.

Jango Fett
BOUNTY HUNTER

Father like son
Though it is based on Jango's appearance in Episode II, this face print was first used for his son, Boba Fett (p.26).

Torso piece with silver Mandalorian armor plates is unique to Jango

Rocket power
Jango's silver jetpack also comes in the 2013 LEGO *Star Wars* Advent Calendar, but Santa Jango does not wear it. It gives a boost to a sleigh instead.

Unique legs and hips have printed straps, pistol holsters, silver armor, and kneepads

DATA FILE

YEAR: 2013
FIRST SET: 75015 Corporate Alliance Tank Droid
NO. OF SETS: 1
PIECES: 6
ACCESSORIES: Twin blasters

STAR VARIANT

Boy Boba

Exclusive to the 2002 Jango Fett's *Slave I* set, the first young Boba has a yellow face with a serious look. His printed torso piece is unique to this variant.

This determined young clone will one day become a great bounty hunter, but for now he is learning combat skills under the guardianship of his father, Jango. Young Boba's minifigure appears alongside his father in Jango Fett's *Slave I* (set 7153) and the 2013 LEGO *Star Wars* Advent Calendar (set 75023). He has short LEGO legs to make him smaller than the Jango minifigure.

Lady locks

The first young Boba has long hair that is typically used on female minifigures. Obi-Wan Kenobi, Luke Skywalker, and Anakin Skywalker have also sported this hair, but Boba was the first LEGO *Star Wars* minifigure to wear it in black.

Only one other minifigure has this hair piece in the LEGO *Star Wars* theme: Ezra Bridger

Boba's head is dual-sided. This side shows him grinning, but the other shows him looking sly

Unique blue torso piece has printing to show wrinkled tunic, exposed skin at neck, and brown belt

This uniform is worn by all young clones studying on Kamino

Half-size legs in this medium blue color also appear on Max Rebo

Boba Fett
YOUNG CLONE

DATA FILE

YEAR: 2013
FIRST SET:
75023 LEGO *Star Wars*
Advent Calendar
NO. OF SETS: 1
PIECES: 4
ACCESSORIES: None

Mandalorian Super Commando
DARTH MAUL'S FOLLOWER

The Mandalorian super commando takes orders from Darth Maul in one LEGO set. The super commando wears traditional Mandalorian armor—but painted to show allegiance to his leader, Darth Maul. Two variants of the super commando minifigure appear in the set, the only difference being the flesh-colored head pieces beneath their helmets.

Handprint painted on helmet as a sign of strength

Mandalorian Speeder (set 75022)
Darth Maul and two faithful Mandalorian super commandos race to take over the planet Mandalore.

Helmet is the same mold as other Mandalorian helmets, but with unique printing

DATA FILE

YEAR: 2013
FIRST SET: 75022
Mandalorian Speeder
NO. OF SETS: 1
PIECES: 5
ACCESSORIES:
Blaster

Uniquely unique
The Mandalorian Speeder (set 75022) is the only LEGO *Star Wars* set to include exclusive minifigures only—Darth Maul with mechanical legs and the Mandalorian super commando.

Pearl gray jetpack also worn by former Mandalorian leader, Pre Vizsla (p. 17)

Armor painted red and black to match Darth Maul's red and black tattoos

STAR VARIANT

Ventress variant

This variant is exclusive to Sith Nightspeeder (set 7957). The printing on Asajj's sleeveless body suit armor continues on the back of her torso and matches her leg design.

From the Outer Rim

A Nightsister from the planet Dathomir, Ventress is not the only Dathomirian minifigure. The famous Sith Lord Darth Maul was a Dathomirian Nightbrother, taken away from his home planet at an early age by Darth Sidious.

Asajj Ventress is a deadly assassin who works for the Sith Lord Count Dooku. Her fearsome minifigure has a unique head and torso, and wields twin red-bladed lightsabers. Asajj has dark side powers and a fiery temper—and she is on a mission to cause trouble in three Clone Wars sets.

Purple tattoo markings are continued on the back of the head

DATA FILE

YEAR: 2015
FIRST SET: 75087
Anakin's Custom Jedi Starfighter
NO. OF SETS: 1
PIECES: 3
ACCESSORIES:
Lightsaber

Unusually, this 2015 Asajj is not based on her appearance in *Star Wars: The Clone Wars*

Unique torso shows Asajj's gray and black body suit

Asajj strides into battle in trousers here, but a 2008 variant wears a black cloth skirt with a unique torso

Asajj wields a red lightsaber. The curved hilt is unique to her minifigure in LEGO *Star Wars*

Asajj Ventress
SITH ASSASSIN

9

Hondo Ohnaka is the fearsome leader of a gang of Weequay pirates. His minifigure wears mismatched clothes, a black bandana, and green-eyed goggles—items he has scavenged on his many journeys. Hondo only appears in one LEGO set, but he and his pilfering gang are always plotting new ways to make a quick buck.

Black bandana is also worn by the Weequay bounty hunter Shahan Alama (p.18)

Pirate Tank (set 7753)
Hondo is the gunner on board the pirate tank in this set. The tank is equipped with flick missiles and a huge blaster cannon. Hondo and his gang of pirates are on a mission to kidnap Obi-Wan—the Jedi Master will fetch a good ransom!

Shoulder epaulets show all the other pirates who's in charge

Epaulet
The LEGO epaulet shoulder piece is worn by several minifigures across other LEGO themes, including pirates and soldiers. In LEGO *Star Wars*, however, only two minifigures wear this piece, Hondo and Embo (p.13).

Hondo's unique head is printed with goggles and Weequay skin

Three other LEGO *Star Wars* minifigures have dark red arms: Chancellor Palpatine, Commander Fox, and the Royal Guard

Hondo Ohnaka
WEEQUAY PIRATE

Torso is printed with an elaborate jacket, which Hondo wears over a ragged white shirt. Hondo thinks the jacket gives him an air of grandeur

DATA FILE

YEAR: 2009
FIRST SET:
7753 Pirate Tank
NO. OF SETS: 1
PIECES: 5
ACCESSORIES: None

Pirate ponytail
Turk's black ponytail is printed on the back of his head—and continues down the back of his torso.

Turk Falso is a tough Weequay criminal. His minifigure is second-in-command in Hondo Ohnaka's pirate gang, and he wears clothes suitable for a pirate's life of planet-hopping and petty thieving. Turk searches for Jedi minifigures to hold for ransom, but he's also out to double-cross his fellow pirates. Luckily for everyone, this rotten pirate only appears in one set.

Turk's headband wraps all the way round the head piece and ties up at the back

DATA FILE

YEAR: 2009
FIRST SET:
7753 Pirate Tank
NO. OF SETS: 1
PIECES: 3
ACCESSORIES:
Twin pistols
ACCESSORIES: None

Unique head piece is printed with Turk's leathery Weequay face

Turk is the only minifigure in the LEGO *Star Wars* theme with dark green arms

Turk carries a pair of ancient pistols

Unique torso is printed on both sides with Turk's tattered clothing and weapon harness

Turk Falso
DANGEROUS PIRATE

Man of weapons
Turk wields many weapons in his crime-filled life. He uses this dark bluish-gray cutlass to threaten Jedi hostages.

Bounty hunter Sugi is honest but deadly. Whether she is sent to capture a Jedi Knight or protect a family of poor farmers, she will not give up until the mission is complete. Sugi's minifigure wears functional clothes that help her get the job done. She doesn't need anything else—apart from her weapons! Sugi carries out many missions, but she only appears in one set.

DATA FILE

YEAR: 2011
FIRST SET: 7930
Bounty Hunter Pursuit
NO. OF SETS: 1
PIECES: 3
ACCESSORIES:
Blaster, vibroblade

Sugi
HONORABLE BOUNTY HUNTER

Sugi is an Iridonian Zabrak. Her head piece has small printed horns and precise face tattoos

The back of Sugi's unique head piece is printed with two more horns and Sugi's purple hair. Her hair is pulled into a neat top knot, so it doesn't get in her minifigure's way during a mission

Sugi's unique torso is printed with her simple red vest and metal necklace—her most treasured possession

Vibroblade vibrates to make it more efficient than a regular blade

Sugi's weapon of choice is an EE-3 carbine rifle

Plain gray pants give Sugi ease of movement in combat

Multifunctional

Embo's multi-purpose hat with traditional Kyuzo markings is a 3x3 inverted radar LEGO piece. The same piece (in black, without special printing) is also used for the Imperial probe droid.

Embo's metal hat can also be thrown as a weapon or used as a shield

Embo is a Kyuzo bounty hunter with sand-green, scaly skin and yellow eyes. He is part of Sugi's team of bounty hunters on board the Bounty Hunter Assault Gunship (set 7930). His minifigure carries a bowcaster and is made up of many unique pieces, including finely detailed hat, head, torso, and leg pieces.

Straps and armor

The back of Embo's torso contains more printed detail, which continues the pattern of his armor and ammo belt.

Epaulets piece is also worn by Hondo Ohnaka (p. 10)

Embo wears a bronze breathing mask to filter moisture out of the air

Modified bowcaster

Unique torso is printed with Embo's sturdy armor and his ammunition strap

Utility belt printed on hip piece

Unique leg piece is printed with Embo's Kyuzo-patterned wrap

DATA FILE

YEAR: 2011
FIRST SET: 7930
Bounty Hunter Pursuit
NO. OF SETS: 1
PIECES: 5
ACCESSORIES:
Bowcaster

Embo
KYUZO BOUNTY HUNTER

The elite assassin droid is the best of the best. Encased in black armor, this skilled assassin can blend into the shadows during a top-secret mission. His tall, thin minifigure has appeared in three LEGO sets since 2009—always in the unsavory company of bounty hunters or other assassin droids.

Orange head sensors enable the elite assassin droid to see in all directions at once

Bounty Hunter Assault Gunship (set 7930)
The elite assassin droid joins bounty hunters Embo, Aurra Sing, and Sugi on board the assault gunship. This villainous group are on the hunt for Jedi that they can capture and lock up in the ship's prison cell.

Cone head piece is unique to assassin droids in LEGO *Star Wars*

Elite Assassin Droid
VILLAIN FOR HIRE

STAR VARIANT
Assassin droid
The regular assassin droid minifigure is exactly the same as the elite assassin droid, apart from his color. The assassin droid is silver, and comes in just one LEGO set, Assassin Droids Battle Pack (set 8015). One of the more famous assassin droids is IG-88 (p.27).

Assassin droid has the same torso piece as the battle droid minifigure and rocket droid commander

Mechanical body covered with blaster-resistant armor

Long-range blaster rifle is perfect for carrying out assassinations without being detected

DATA FILE
YEAR: 2009
FIRST SET: 8015 Assassin Droids Battle Pack
NO. OF SETS: 3
PIECES: 1
ACCESSORIES: Blaster

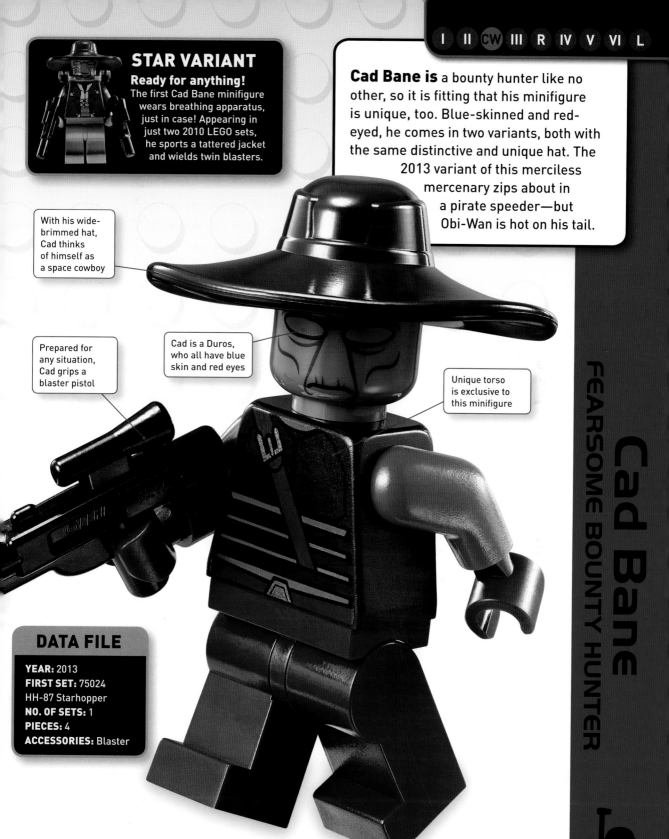

STAR VARIANT
Ready for anything!
The first Cad Bane minifigure wears breathing apparatus, just in case! Appearing in just two 2010 LEGO sets, he sports a tattered jacket and wields twin blasters.

Cad Bane is a bounty hunter like no other, so it is fitting that his minifigure is unique, too. Blue-skinned and red-eyed, he comes in two variants, both with the same distinctive and unique hat. The 2013 variant of this merciless mercenary zips about in a pirate speeder—but Obi-Wan is hot on his tail.

With his wide-brimmed hat, Cad thinks of himself as a space cowboy

Prepared for any situation, Cad grips a blaster pistol

Cad is a Duros, who all have blue skin and red eyes

Unique torso is exclusive to this minifigure

Cad Bane
FEARSOME BOUNTY HUNTER

DATA FILE
YEAR: 2013
FIRST SET: 75024 HH-87 Starhopper
NO. OF SETS: 1
PIECES: 4
ACCESSORIES: Blaster

The Mandalorian is a deadly soldier from the planet Mandalore. He owns many weapons, but his distinctive blue and gray armor is his most treasured possession. Appearing in only two LEGO sets, the Mandalorian's minifigure joins forces with the Separatists—even though his sturdy armor was the inspiration for clone trooper armor!

Mandalorian Battle Pack (set 7914)
Four armored Mandalorian minifigures attack the clone army in this LEGO set. They are equipped with a speeder and a variety of weapons, including a blaster turret, long-range rifle, and blasters.

Helmet has similar markings to Jango Fett's helmet (p.6)

DATA FILE
YEAR: 2011
FIRST SET: 7914
Mandalorian Battle Pack
NO. OF SETS: 2
PIECES: 5
ACCESSORIES:
Long or short blaster

Jetpack fits around minifigure's neck

Mandalorians are trained to use a variety of weapons

Under the helmet
Beneath the Mandalorian's helmet is a unique LEGO head piece printed with blue eyes and pale features.

Mandalorian ARMORED WARRIOR

Jetpack
The Mandalorian's armor is fitted with a jetpack. Jango Fett (p.6) also wears a jetpack, which is sometimes attached to his helmet.

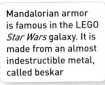

Mandalorian armor is famous in the LEGO *Star Wars* galaxy. It is made from an almost indestructible metal, called beskar

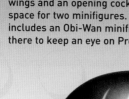

Pre Vizsla's Mandalorian Fighter (set 9525)
Pre Vizsla's plane has rotating wings and an opening cockpit with space for two minifigures. This set includes an Obi-Wan minifigure, there to keep an eye on Pre Vizsla.

This helmet piece features green trident-shaped printing

Cape
Pre Vizsla's cape is technically a pauldron cloth, designed to protect his shoulder and upper arm. Over that fits a jet pack with twin nozzles.

Sand blue cape with Mandalorian symbol on the back

Governor of Concordia turned leader of the renegade Death Watch organization, Pre Vizsla has appeared just once as a minifigure, in 2012. Beneath his impressive helmet is a stern face with cheek lines and high brow pattern that also appears on a Mandalorian super commando. Pre Vizsla is wielder of a rare darksaber, which was stolen from the Jedi in ancient times.

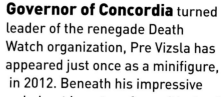

Pre Vizsla
CAPED CONSPIRATOR

The only other minifigure with this Darksaber is Darth Maul, who carries it in the Mandalorian Speeder (set 75022)

Unique torso and leg pieces, printed with Mandalorian armor

DATA FILE

YEAR: 2012
FIRST SET:
9525 Pre Vizsla's Mandalorian Fighter
NO. OF SETS: 1
PIECES: 6
ACCESSORIES: Darksaber

Shahan Alama was a pirate—until he was kicked out of the gang for being too nasty! Now he is a bounty hunter who works with Cad Bane. His mismatched clothing and bandana point to his former life as a pirate, but Shahan's mean streak runs deep so he feels right at home among Bane's gang of hired brutes. Fortunately, Shahan wreaks havoc in just one LEGO set.

DATA FILE

YEAR: 2010
FIRST SET: 8128
Cad Bane's Speeder
NO. OF SETS: 1
PIECES: 4
ACCESSORIES: Blaster

Dark red bandana hat piece is unique to Shahan. Hondo Ohnaka wears it in black (p.10)

Protective chestplate worn around the neck

Shahan's armor
Shahan's chestplate is printed on the back of his torso, too. Working together with Cad Bane has its risks!

Shahan's unique head piece is printed with a savage expression and a Weequay skin pattern, which continues on the back

Pearl gold arm was taken from a combat droid to replace Shahan's destroyed right arm

Belt was stolen from a Twi'lek nobleman

Shahan Alama
PIRATE TURNED BOUNTY HUNTER

Shahan has a blaster—and is not afraid to use it!

Weequay skin
There are four Weequay minifigures: Shahan, Hondo Ohnaka (p. 10), the Weequay Skiff Guard, and Turk Falso (p.11). They all have faces printed with Weequay skin, but the patterns and colors vary from one villain to the next.

Bounty Hunter
Assault Gunship (set 7930)

Aurra Sing knows exactly what will fetch the highest ransom. In this set, she's managed to get hold of a Jedi holocron! Aurra's minifigure stores it in a secret chamber aboard the bounty hunter gunship.

Weapons vest

The back of Aurra's unique torso is printed with her brown vest, in which she stores compact weapons and extra ammo.

Ruthless bounty hunter Aurra Sing will stop at nothing to get her prize. Her fearless minifigure is dressed in an orange jumpsuit laden with weapons, but wears no armor! Aurra appears in just one set and her minifigure is almost completely built out of unique pieces— only her arms and hands can be found on other minifigures.

Long brown hair is tied up, out of the way

Unique hairstyle

Aurra's long, brown LEGO hair piece was specially designed for her 2011 minifigure. It fits into the stud on top of Aurra's otherwise bald head piece and flows neatly down her back.

Unique head piece is printed with Aurra's bright green eyes and confident smile

Utility belt

Aurra's orange jumpsuit is functional. It allows her to maneuver easily during combat

Unique leg pieces are printed with holsters for Aurra's twin pistols

Aurra Sing
RELENTLESS BOUNTY HUNTER

DATA FILE

YEAR: 2011
FIRST SET: 7133
Bounty Hunter Pursuit
NO. OF SETS: 1
PIECES: 4
ACCESSORIES:
Twin blasters

Savage Opress is on a secret mission. Hired by Asajj Ventress to destroy Count Dooku, his minifigure poses as Dooku's new apprentice. Savage appears in just one LEGO set, where his horned, Dathomirian minifigure must decide who to attack: the Jedi Anakin Skywalker, or his two despised Sith Masters?

Savage Opress DARK APPRENTICE

Dathomir Speeder (set 7957)
Asajj Ventress, a Nightsister from Savage's home planet of Dathomir, pilots a Nightspeeder with Savage in this set.

LEGO spear piece with ax head attached

Enchanted blade is a weapon from a clan of witches called the Nightsisters

Savage's Zabrak head piece is the same mold as Darth Maul's horned head piece (p.4), but with yellow markings in a different pattern

Nightbrother tattoos on yellow skin

Savage's fellow Dathomirian, Darth Maul, also wields a double-bladed lightsaber

Unique armor piece fits over the minifigure's neck. The Dathomirian armor protects Savage's torso and shoulders

DATA FILE

YEAR: 2011
FIRST SET: 7957 Sith Nightspeeder
NO. OF SETS: 1
PIECES: 5
ACCESSORIES: Double-bladed lightsaber, enchanted blade

Head piece has similar printing to previous variants, but a unique, smug expression

Eyes are yellow, ringed with red

Darth Maul's minifigure was last seen plummeting down an exhaust shaft on Naboo. Now, his fifth variant has returned with new mechanical legs, replacing the LEGO parts that were dispatched by Obi-Wan's lightsaber. Maul is exceptionally proud of his new legs, which are unique to his minifigure. He also wields the Darksaber.

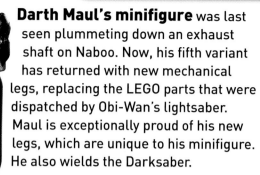

Rare printed arms, depicting yet more tattoos

Only one other minifigure wields the Darksaber, Mandalorian soldier, Pre Vizsla

New, shirtless look gives Maul the opportunity to display his Nightbrother tattoos

Darth Maul
CYBORG SITH

No more robes
Darth Maul's latest minifigure is the second one to feature Maul's shirtless torso. This new torso, however, has new printed details, including a silver collar and all-silver belt.

Mechanical legs
Darth Maul's unique leg pieces clip onto his unique hip piece. Although the LEGO mold makes the legs appear hinged, they are each a single piece of plastic.

Clawed feet make mechanical Maul look even more deadly

DATA FILE

YEAR: 2013
FIRST SET: 75022 Mandalorian Speeder
NO. OF SETS: 1
PIECES: 6
ACCESSORIES: Twin lightsabers

Ruthless bounty hunter

Rako Hardeen is really Obi-Wan Kenobi in disguise! He is undercover to infiltrate Cad Bane's crew and find out his plans. While there have been many Obi-Wan minifigures, this is the first of his Hardeen identity. The tattoos on his face show the tribal allegiances of the original Hardeen, who came from the planet Concord Dawn.

Rako Hardeen
JEDI IN DISGUIDE

Speeder
Rako is pictured here on the pirate speeder that comes with this minifigure in the HH-87 Starhopper (set 75024).

New face print with distinctive tattoo is unique to this minifigure

Rako's back
The back of the head is a light flesh color. A printed brown curve suggests the bulge at the back of the shaven skull.

Sniper rifle is extended with lightsaber hilt piece

This is the first minifigure to feature this new torso print

Metallic gold printed knee pads

DATA FILE

YEAR: 2013
FIRST SET: 75024 HH-87 Starhopper
NO. OF SETS: 1
PIECES: 3
ACCESSORIES: Sniper rifle

Mos Eisley Cantina (set 75052)
This labyrinthine saloon on Tatooine is the setting for the confrontation between Greedo and Han Solo. The pair discuss Han's unpaid debts at a table in a shady alcove.

Rodian bounty hunter

Greedo is looking for Han Solo to recover money owed to his boss, Jabba the Hutt. He has finally caught up with Han in the raucous Mos Eisley Cantina (set 75052) on Tatooine. There's going to be a showdown—but will greedy Greedo persuade Han Solo to settle his debt?

STAR VARIANT

First Greedo
The first Greedo minifigure appears only in the 2004 Mos Eisley Cantina (set 4501). With his exclusive dark-turquoise head, he is highly sought after by LEGO *Star Wars* collectors.

First Rodian
Greedo was the first Rodian minifigure. His pimpled head-mold was designed just for him, but later used in other colors for fellow Rodians W. Wald and Onaconda Farr. LEGO designers updated Greedo's own head printing for the 2014 variant.

Large disc-shaped eyes with light reflectors

Sand-green head is unique to this Greedo

Unique hips have printed silver belt, while legs have printed low-slung brown belt

Tan vest over sky-blue jumpsuit

DATA FILE

YEAR: 2014
FIRST SET: 75052
Mos Eisley Cantina
NO. OF SETS: 1
PIECES: 3
ACCESSORIES:
Blaster

Greedo
BOUNTY HUNTER

This terrifying Trandoshan bounty hunter made his minifigure debut alongside redesigns of Boba Fett and Han Solo in 2010's *Slave I* (set 8097), although he doesn't actually have a place to sit aboard the LEGO starship! Bossk's reptilian head, complete with smooth horns and sharp teeth, was specially cast for this dangerous LEGO minifigure.

Flying in style
Bossk's flight suit has intricate details on the back as well as the front.

Slave I (set 8097)
Bossk helps his fellow bounty hunter Boba Fett to capture Han Solo inside a block of carbonite in this 2010 set. Bossk doesn't have a seat aboard Fett's starship, *Slave I*, but he can fit beneath the cabin during flight.

Painted infrared-vision eyes

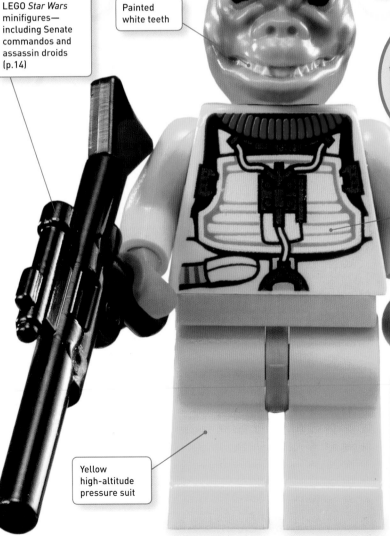

A blaster rifle is the weapon of choice for many LEGO *Star Wars* minifigures—including Senate commandos and assassin droids (p.14)

Painted white teeth

Unique sand-green head is made from hard ABS plastic

Bossk's body
The torso design on Bossk's flight suit is unique to him. It is more detailed than the flight suit sported by rebel pilots Luke Skywalker, Dutch Vander, Biggs Darklighter, Wedge Antilles and Dak Ralter.

White flak vest

Bossk
ALIEN BOUNTY HUNTER

Yellow high-altitude pressure suit

DATA FILE
YEAR: 2010
FIRST SET: 8097 *Slave I*
NO. OF SETS: 2
PIECES: 3
ACCESSORIES: Blaster rifle

DATA FILE

YEAR: 2011
FIRST SET: 10221
Super Star Destroyer
NO. OF SETS: 1
PIECES: 2
ACCESSORIES: Blaster rifle

Dengar once suffered a severe head injury. Imperial agents fixed most of the damage, but Dengar always wears a head bandage

This minifigure might wear makeshift armor, but don't underestimate him! Dengar is a dangerous bounty hunter. He is hired by Darth Vader to capture the *Millennium Falcon* and its passengers. Two variants of Dengar appear in two LEGO *Star Wars* sets, both with his huge Valken-38 blaster rifle close at hand.

Scarred face from a swoop-racer crash

STAR VARIANT

Ninja bandage
The 2006 Dengar variant comes with the LEGO set *Slave I* (set 6209). His torso and legs are different and the minifigure's standard LEGO head piece is covered with a white Ninja hood.

Dengar painted his armor brown

Dengar's armor is built from discarded Imperial materials. It includes pieces of armor from sandtroopers, snowtroopers, and stormtroopers

White gloves to protect hands

Dengar
BANDAGED BOUNTY HUNTER

Bounty hunters
Most of the bounty hunters hired by Darth Vader to track down the rebels can be found in LEGO *Star Wars* sets. Bossk, Dengar, Boba Fett (p.26), and IG-88 (p.27) have all been made into LEGO minifigures. Only Zuckuss and 4-LOM remain elusive.

Mandalorian bounty

hunter Boba Fett appears in 12 LEGO *Star Wars* sets, with 10 distinct variations. Boba's latest incarnation is battle-worn, but equipped with all he needs to catch his quarry: a probing rangefinder, a powerful jetpack, and unbeatable firepower.

Blue-gray detachable rangefinder fits into a hole in Boba's helmet

Gray markings are battle damage

Boba Fett
BOUNTY HUNTER

DATA FILE

YEAR: 2015
FIRST SET: 75060
Slave I
NO. OF SETS: 1
PIECES: 7
ACCESSORIES: Modified rifle, cape

Wookiee hair is worn as a prize

Unique new leg printing

STAR VARIANTS

Bronze Boba
There are only two of these solid bronze Boba Fetts in existence. One was given away to a lucky competition winner as part of the LEGO "May the Fourth" promotion in 2010.

Cloud City
This is the first Boba variant to have leg and arm printing and is unique to Cloud City (set 10123), released in 2003. A similar variant with plain gray legs and arms was released in 2000.

New trousers
This 2010 Boba Fett is the first to feature blue legs. The pale blue part features in three later variants, all of which have additional printing.

Tattered fabric pauldron cloth is unique to Boba Fett

EXCLUSIVE

Cover star
Available only with this book, this white Boba Fett variant is based on original concept designs for the character. A 2010 variant with the first Boba helmet mold has a simpler white look.

Cone-shaped head has motion, sound, and heat sensors that help IG-88 catch his prey

IG-88 has individual orange sensors on his silver head plate. Pre-2011 variants of his minifigure have a translucent orange round plate piece

Assassin droid IG-88 stalks the LEGO *Star Wars* galaxy in three sets, and in each one he has a slightly different look—though each is as intimidating as the last. The monstrous minifigure is obsessed with hunting and killing, and he comes well equipped to pursue his passion. His round, sensor-filled head can see in all directions at once!

STAR VARIANTS

Silver assassin
This metallic silver variant of IG-88 appears in *Slave I* (set 6209), released in 2006. He carries an older version of a LEGO *Star Wars* blaster.

White assassin
This white droid appears on the LEGO Death Star (set 10188). He is thought to be a variant of IG-88, but he is not named as him on the set box.

IG-88's body is made up of identical pieces to the LEGO battle droid

IG-88 holds a weapon in each hand—this one is a medium blaster

One of IG-88's hands is at a 90 degree angle to his opposite hand so he can hold his blaster vertically

DATA FILE

YEAR: 2011
FIRST SET: 10221 Super Star Destroyer
NO. OF SETS: 1
PIECES: 7
ACCESSORIES: Blaster rifle, blaster

IG-88
BOUNTY HUNTER

DK | Penguin Random House

Editors Pamela Afram, Hannah Dolan, Clare Hibbert, Shari Last, Julia March, Victoria Taylor, Ellie Barton, Matt Jones, Clare Millar, and Rosie Peet
Designers Elena Jarmoskaite, Pamela Shiels, Mark Richards, Anne Sharples, Jon Hall, and Stefan Georgiou
Senior Designers Jo Connor, and David McDonald
Senior Slipcase Designer Mark Penfound
Pre-Production Producer Kavita Varma
Senior Producer Lloyd Robertson
Managing Editor Paula Regan
Design Manager Guy Harvey
Creative Manager Sarah Harland
Art Director Lisa Lanzarini
Publisher Julie Ferris
Publishing Director Simon Beecroft

Consultants Jon Hall and Ace Kim
Additional minifigures photographed by Gary Ombler

First American Edition, 2016
Publsihed in the United States by
DK Publishing 345 Hudson Street,
New York, New York 10014
DK, a Division of Penguin Random
House LLC

Contains content previously
published in LEGO® *Star Wars*™
*Character Encyclopedia, Updated
and Expanded* (2015)

Page design copyright © 2016
Dorling Kindersley Limited

002–298872–Jan/17

A catalog record for this book is
available from the Library of Congress.

ISBN 978-5-0010-1392-1

Printed in China

www.LEGO.com/starwars
www.dk.com

A WORLD OF IDEAS:
SEE ALL THERE IS TO KNOW

Dorling Kindersley would like to thank:
Randi Sørensen, Robert Stefan Ekblom, Paul Hansford,
Heike Bornhausen, and Jakob Liesenfeld at the LEGO Group;
J.W. Rinzler and Leland Chee at Lucasfilm; Julia March,
Beth Davies, and Toby Mann for editorial assistance; Mik Gates,
Akiko Kato, Jon Hall, and Jane Ewart for design assistance.